Editor

Eric Migliaccio

Managing Editor

Ina Massler Levin, M.A.

Editor-in-Chief

Sharon Coan, M.S. Ed.

Illustrator

Blanca Apodaca

Cover Artist

Denise Bauer

Art Coordinator

Kevin Barnes

Art Director

CJae Froshay

Imaging

Craig Gunnell

Product Manager

Phil Garcia

Publisher

Mary D,. Smith, M.S. Ed.

B. Richards

D0472916

Quips, Quotes, & Queries

Artwork © Susan Winget

Author

Sylvia Barrett

Teacher Created Resources, Inc.

6421 Industry Way

Westminster, CA 92683

www.teachercreated.com

ISBN: 978-0-7439-3508-1

©2003 Teacher Created Resources, Inc.

Reprinted, 2010

Made in U.S.A.

Introduction

The three sections of *Quips, Quotes, & Queries* are packed with an array of activities designed to guide the student into higher-leveled thinking. The majority of the activities are open-ended; thus, making the materials adaptable for a wide range of ages. All three sections follow a similar format, but each section is different and demands a graduating level of ability. To truly develop higher thinking skills, it is advised to begin with Section 1 and progress through Section 3.

Quips, Quotes, & Queries should be an independent activity. This allows each student to develop his/her thinking skills. If the student does not achieve every item in a lesson, the closing discussion gives the opportunity to learn and "piggy back" ideas. Students should always feel free to be risk takers; consequently, all reasonable responses should be accepted for open-ended questions. The teacher can then direct the discussion in such a manner that the most desirable conclusions are reached. Always encourage the student to think "outside the box," that is, to think about things from unique and unexpected perspectives.

Suggestions For Use

Activities may best be completed in this order:

1. A sponge or beginning activity to engage the student's thinking skills

2. An activity that provides differentiation and extension for individual needs

3. A station activity for selected students with idea sharing in a small group after completion

4. A weekly extension class activity with an end of the week closure and discussion

5. Individual page items could be given to students orally or visually as a quick thinking activity

This is the first of three sections and the foundation for the sections to follow. As the student begins here and works through the sections, he/she will develop the ability to think in a high and creative manner. Below are listed the topics covered in Section 1.

- **Quote of the Day**—This gives a quick lesson in wisdom for living and often offers the student experience in understanding analogies and abstract ideas.

- **Rules of Grammar**—This includes parts of speech and their correct usage.

- **Flexible Thinking**—This is thinking about things in unusual, unique, and unexpected ways. Sometimes this may be referred to as "outside the box" thinking.

- **Fluent Thinking**—Thinking fluently means generating many and varied ideas. The more ideas, the more fluent the thinking.

- **Forced Association**—Comparing two unlike things will cause the student to think more deeply and find obscure similarities.

- **Rhyme & Poetry**—Learning how to use figurative speech and create a rhythm pattern allows students to express themselves creatively and vividly.

- **Reversed Thinking**—Thinking in reverse gives students the skills needed for problem solving. This can also offer thought for how a reversed situation could change the outcome.

- **Proverbs**—This is another source of quick lessons in wisdom and understanding analogies.

- **Math/Geometry**—Many math concepts are covered as exposure or review.

- **Synonyms/Homonyms**—Practice with words that mean the same or sound the same gives opportunity for familiarizing students with words and their proper usage.

- **Abbreviations**—Activities provide students with practice in using abbreviated forms.

- **General Knowledge**—Basic knowledge questions in varied areas create curiosity in students to search out even more information about subjects of their interest.

- **Word Play**—The Funnies at the end of each page will create the ability to play with words, as students *create a new and different answer* to the riddle.

- **Groups**—There are pairs and triplets, as well as animal group names.

- **Introspective Thought**—Looking inward gives the student an opportunity to set personal goals or to realize reasons for what he/she thinks or feels.

Ready, Set, Think: #1

Quote of the Day

"The chains of habit are generally too small to be
felt until they are too strong to be broken."

~ Anonymous

↪ Tell what you think this means: _____

_____

↪ What is a good habit of yours? _____

_____

↪ What is a habit you would like to change?_____

_____

Rules of Grammar

A *sentence* is a group of words expressing a complete thought. A sentence should always
start with a _____ letter. A sentence should always have ending punctuation.

↪ Why did I not tell you what kind of punctuation should be at the end of a sentence?

_____

_____

↪ Write one very good sentence. _____

_____

_____

Question of the Day

↪ What color is a bad grade? _____

↪ Explain. _____

_____

The Funnies

↪ What is the funniest thing that ever happened to you? _____

_____

_____

Quote of the Day

"Minds are like parachutes—they work best when open."

~ Anonymous

➥ What do you think this quote means? _____

_____

➥ Think of a time when your mind was a closed parachute. Briefly describe that time.

_____

_____

_____

➥ Now think of a time when your mind was an open parachute. Describe that time.

_____

_____

_____

Rules of Grammar

A *noun* is a word for a person, place, or thing.

Examples: <u>Ann</u> lives in <u>Boston</u>.   Work brings <u>success</u>.   <u>Students</u> attend <u>school</u>.

➥ Write a sentence in which you use a noun for a person, a place, or a thing.

Circle the nouns in your sentence._____

_____

Animal Parade

Make a list of six animals. Each animal's name must begin with the last letter of the previous animal. You may not use an animal more than once in your parade.

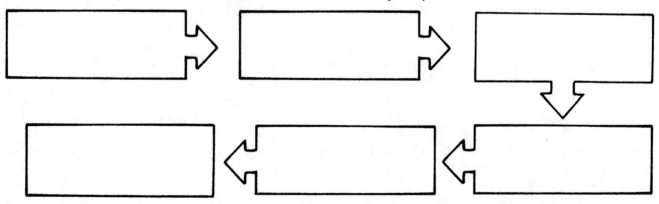

The Funnies

➥ What kind of bird is always around when there is something to eat or drink?

Your Creative Answer: _____

Quote of the Day

"Wonder implies the desire to learn."

~ Aristotle

⇒ What do you think this quote means? _____

_____

⇒ Why would this be a true statement?_____

_____

⇒ Who was Aristotle?_____

_____

Rules of Grammar

A *pronoun* is a word used to take the place of a noun. Using pronouns helps prevent the repeating and overuse of names. If a pronoun takes the place of a noun, let's review what a noun is.

⇒ A noun names a _____, _____, or _____.

⇒ List as many pronouns as you can. _____

_____

⇒ Write a sentence that uses a pronoun. _____

_____

Comparisons

⇒ How is your home like a matchbox? _____

_____

_____

Rhyme Time

⇒ List as many words as possible that rhyme with *leak*. _____

_____

⇒ Now think of one rhyming word for *leak* that you think no one else will list. _____

⇒ On the back of this paper, write a 3- or 4-line poem using some of your rhyming words for the end of your poem lines.

The Funnies

⇒ Where do butchers dance?

Your Creative Answer: _____

Ready, Set, Think: #4

Quote of the Day

"Genius is one percent inspiration and ninety-nine percent perspiration."

~ Thomas Edison

→ What does this quote mean to you? _____

_____

→ What do you know about Thomas Edison? _____

_____

→ Do you think that Thomas Edison may have used this belief in his own life? Explain.

_____

Rules of Grammar

A *verb* is a word that expresses action, being, or state of being.

Examples: That man <u>is</u> a banker. Helen <u>painted</u> a picture.

A verb may be made up of several words, and then it is called a *verb phrase.*

Example: This book <u>should have been sent</u> to the library.

→ Write a sentence with an action verb: _____

_____

→ Write a sentence with a state-of-being verb: _____

_____

→ Write a sentence with a verb phrase: _____

_____

What's the Question?

→ The answer is "a hexagon." Write two questions for which this could be the answer.

1. _____

2. _____

Collections

→ What is the name for a group of each of these animals?

ants _____   lions _____

hogs _____   partridges _____

The Funnies

→ What do you call the person who mows the grass on a baseball field?

Your Creative Answer: _____

Ready, Set, Think: #5

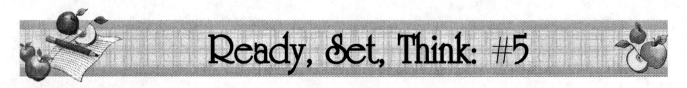

Quote of the Day

"You can't build a reputation on what you are going to do."

~ Henry Ford

- What does this quote mean to you? ______________________________

____

- For what is Henry Ford famous? ______________________________

____

- Do you think he had to work hard on his invention? Explain your answer. ____________

Rules of Grammar

An *adjective* is used to describe or modify a noun or pronoun. An adjective may be a single word, a phrase, or a clause.

Examples: We saw beautiful valleys and rugged mountains. *(single words)*

The rug on the floor is blue. *(phrase)*

The man who spoke is a teacher. *(clause)*

- If an adjective can be used to describe a noun, tell what a noun is. ____________

____

- What is a pronoun? ______________________________
- Write a sentence that uses single word adjectives. Circle your adjective(s). ____________

____

Can You Finish These?

- Finish these sayings:

A stitch in time ____________ Haste makes ____________

An apple a day ____________ Penny wise ____________

Birds of a feather ____________ Still water ____________

A Sentence to Complete

- Sometimes, I daydream about ______________________________

____

The Funnies

- Why are garbage men unhappy?

Your Creative Answer: ______________________________

Ready, Set, Think: #6

Quote of the Day

"Imagination is more important than knowledge."
~ Albert Einstein

• What is imagination? _____

• What is knowledge? _____

• Do you feel this quote is true? Explain your answer. _____

_____

• Who was Albert Einstein? _____

_____

Rules of Grammar

An *adverb* is used to describe a verb, an adjective, or another adverb (for example, She sang <u>beautifully</u>). Many times adverbs will end in *ly*, but not always.

• Write a sentence using at least one adverb. _____

_____

Let's Celebrate

• There are at least 16 holidays and fun celebrations in October. How many can you name?_____

_____

Wake Up Call

• If you woke up and you were a musical instrument, which one would you want to be? Why? _____

_____

• List at least eight good study habits that every student should practice.

1. _____   5. _____

2. _____   6. _____

3. _____   7. _____

4. _____   8. _____

The Funnies

• What do you get when you cross a mouse and a lion?

Your Creative Answer: _____

_____

Quote of the Day

"Keep your face in the sunshine and you cannot see the shadow."

~ Helen Keller

➡ What do you think this quote is saying? _____

_____

➡ What do you know about Helen Keller?_____

_____

➡ Why is this an interesting quote to have been said by Helen Keller? _____

_____

Rules of Grammar

A *conjunction* connects words or groups of words.

Examples: Bob <u>and</u> Nell are here.   She came <u>but</u> she did not stay.

➡ Write a good sentence using a conjunction. _____

_____

Draw These

Draw the shapes in the boxes to the right.

hexagon	cube	pentagon
parallelogram	trapezoid	octagon

Synonyms

A *synonym* is a word that means the same or nearly the same as another word.

➡ Give three synonyms for each of the words listed below.

said   1. _____   2. _____   3. _____

end   1. _____   2. _____   3. _____

wet   1. _____   2. _____   3. _____

walk   1. _____   2. _____   3. _____

help   1. _____   2. _____   3. _____

The Funnies

➡ What is the first thing that ghosts do when they get in the car?

Your Creative Answer: _____

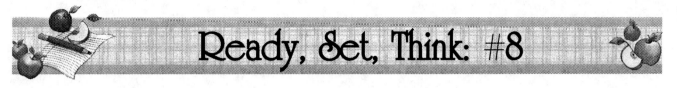

Ready, Set, Think: #8

Quote of the Day

"No man is an island."

~ John Donne

• What is the definition of the word *island*? _____

_____

• Does this quote mean no man is surrounded by water? What does it mean?_____

_____

Rules of Grammar

An *interjection* expresses strong feeling. The interjection has no grammatical relation to the rest of the sentence.

Example: Help! Help!

• Write a three-sentence thought. Use at least one interjection._____

_____

_____

Abbreviations

• Write the abbreviation for each of the words listed below.

pound	_____	quart	_____
kilometer	_____	street	_____
ounce	_____	boulevard	_____
inch	_____	Texas	_____
avenue	_____	Thursday	_____

• What do these abbreviations mean?

R.S.V.P. _____

C.S.T. _____

Ltd. _____

mph_____

The Funnies

• Why didn't the skeleton kid want to go to school?

   Your Creative Answer: _____

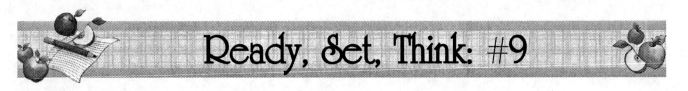

Ready, Set, Think: #9

Quote of the Day

"Music is the international language of mankind."
~ Henry Wadsworth Longfellow

- How can music be a language?_____
- What does universal mean? _____
- What does this quote mean? _____
- Who was Henry Wadsworth Longfellow? _____

Rules of Grammar

- Let's review. Write a brief definition for each of these below.

Noun: _____

Pronoun: _____

Verb: _____

Adjective: _____

Adverb: _____

Conjunction: _____

Interjection: _____

Roman Numerals

- Write the Roman Numeral for each of the numbers below.

10 = _____   50 = _____   49 = _____

1 = _____   100 = _____   99 = _____

5 = _____   19 = _____   2 = _____

Math Trivia

- How many dots are there on a die? _____
- How many degrees in a circle? _____
- Can there be two right angles in a triangle?_____
- How many degrees in a right angle? _____
- What does the word *perimeter* mean? _____

The Funnies

- What musical instrument does a skeleton play?

Your Creative Answer: _____

Ready, Set, Think: #10

Quote of the Day

*"Happiness does not depend upon who you are or what you have;
it depends solely on what you think."*

~ Dale Carnegie

➻ What does this quote say to you? _____

_____

➻ How could you use this thought to help you? _____

_____

Rules of Grammar

Do not confuse the verbs *may* and *can*. *May* is used to ask permission, and *can* refers to ability. (*Examples:* May I go to the movies?   Can the bird fly?)

➻ Write two sentences, one with *may* and one with *can*. _____

_____

_____

Question of the Day

➻ What might a clipboard ask a mousetrap?_____

_____

_____

More Questions

➻ How many years in a decade? _____

➻ How many years in a century? _____

➻ How many years in a millennium? _____

➻ When will we enter the next millennium? _____

➻ What does A.D. stand for in our date? _____

The Funnies

➻ What do you call cattle that sit on the grass?

Your Creative Answer: _____

Ready, Set, Think: #11

Quote of the Day

"A problem well stated is a problem half solved."
~ Charles Kettering

➤ What does this quote mean? _____

_____

➤ How are some ways this truth might help you? _____

_____

Rules of Grammar

Do not misuse the words *good* and *well*. Good is an adjective and must describe a person, place, or thing (a noun). The word *well* is an adverb and must describe a verb, adjective, or another adverb.

Example: Bill is a good writer. *Writer* is a noun, so *good* can describe it.

Example: Bill writes well. Now, *well* describes *write*, a verb.

➤ Adjectives answer the questions *which*, *what kind*, and *how many*. Which one of these questions does *good* answer in the example sentence? _____

➤ Adverbs answer *how*, *when*, *where*. Which question does *well* answer in the example sentence? _____

➤ Write one correct sentence using *good* and another using *well*.

  1. _____

  2. _____

Writing Poetry

➤ Let's write a rhyming poem today. It should have a pattern of rhyme: AABB, ABBA, ABAB, or AAAB. You need to have at least 4 lines, but you may have more. Remember to repeat your pattern. (Choose any topic, and it can be funny.) Be prepared to share.

_____

_____

_____

_____

The Funnies

➤ What does an invisible baby drink?

  Your Creative Answer: _____

Quote of the Day

"People are lonely because they build walls instead of bridges."

~ Cicero

• This quote is a type of analogy. Why would building walls instead of bridges make someone lonely? _____

_____

• What kind of walls could they be building? _____

_____

• What kinds of bridges? _____

• How might you try to build a bridge today? _____

_____

Rules of Grammar

Be sure you are always using the correct form of these two words: *its* and *it's*. Its is the possessive form of *it*. It does not have an apostrophe because pronouns do not use an apostrophe when forming their possessive form. *It's* is a contraction for *it is*. The apostrophe stands for the letter *i* that is left out.

• Write one correct sentence using *its* and another one using *it's*.

1. _____

2. _____

Try This:

• Write a sentence of *at least five words* in which every word starts with the letter *t*.

_____

This is Corny

• Every answer will have the word *corn* in it somewhere.

A horn of plenty _____

Where two streets meet _____

An instrument that looks like a trumpet _____

The outer covering of the eyeball _____

You serve this with cabbage _____

Question for the Day

• Would you rather your best friend be honest, loyal, or rich? Explain your answer.

_____

_____

The Funnies

• What did the wig say to the head?

Your Creative Answer: _____

Ready, Set, Think: #13

Quote of the Day

"Sometimes you have to be silent to be heard."
~ Swiss proverb

➥ How could this be a true statement? _____

_____

➥ Give an example of how this could be true at school. _____

_____

Rules of Grammar

Be careful how you use the word *me*. It can never be the subject of a sentence. The subject of a sentence is who or what the sentence is about. For instance, you would not say, "Me doesn't have any money." Therefore, you still should not say that when you add another name such as "Me and Mary don't have any money." Instead, you should say, "Mary and I don't have any money." Notice *me* changes to *I* and then finds its place after *Mary*. When combined with a noun (Mary), *I* should always come second. In normal sentence structure, this situation will always come before the verb. We will cover the rules next about what you do when it comes after the verb.

➥ Write a correct sentence using *I* combined with another noun as the compound subject.

_____

_____

Fill in the Chart

Female	Male	Offspring
goose		
		calf
	buck	
ewe		
		piglet

The Funnies

➥ Why doesn't St. Nicholas shave?

Your Creative Answer: _____

_____

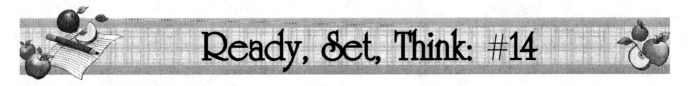

Ready, Set, Think: #14

Quote of the Day

"If you always tell the truth, you never have to rely on your memory."

~ Anonymous

➥ What does this mean? _____

_____

➥ Can you think of an example where this was true? _____

_____

➥ How can you use this quote to help you? _____

_____

Rules of Grammar

Using *me* correctly: *me* is what language experts call the *objective case*. This means it must always receive the action. Usually, this means it will come after the verb.

Examples: He sent *me* a letter.   Please, give *Mary and me* a dollar to spend at the store.
Notice the pronoun *me* follows the noun, *Mary*.

➥ Write a sentence using *me* correctly. Then write a sentence in which you combine *me* with a noun.

1.   _____

_____

2.   _____

_____

A Millennium

➥ What are some changes that must occur when you change millenniums? List as many as you can. _____

_____

Famous Threes

➥ Where do we find these fabled threesomes?

Animals with poor vision   _____

Goldilocks' friends _____

Taking bridge tolls _____

Building homes _____

The Funnies

➥ Why did the butcher put bells on his scale?

Your Creative Answer: _____

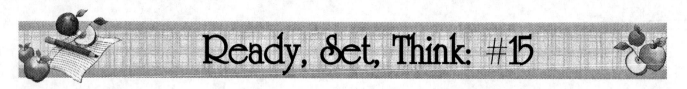

Quote of the Day

*"You cannot do a kindness too soon, because you
never know how soon it will be too late."*
~ Anonymous

�➤ What do you think this quote is saying? _____

_____

➤ Have you ever waited too late to be kind? Can you give an example? _____

_____

Rules of Grammar

An *appositive* is a word, a phrase, or a clause placed near a noun to explain it. An appositive is usually set off with commas.

Example: Mrs. Jones, *my teacher*, writes books.

➤ Use an appositive in an original, well-developed sentence. _____

_____

Forest Fun

➤ What tree reminds you of each phrase?

A person that is old: _____

Something that stretches: _____

A bright color: _____

A nut: _____

A small insect: _____

Another name for cleaning up: _____

A present for the teacher: _____

The remains of a burned object: _____

To yearn: _____

What If?

➤ What if snow were purple? _____

_____

The Funnies

➤ What would you call a knight caught in a windstorm?
Your Creative Answer: _____

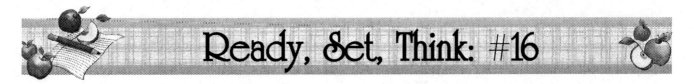

Quote of the Day

*"When something's gone wrong, it's better to talk about
who's going to fix it than who's to blame."*
~ Anonymous

➥ What is the truth found in this quote? _____

_____

➥ What is a situation at school where you have seen students more interested in placing
the blame rather than trying to fix the problem? _____

_____

➥ How could you help when a situation such as above is happening? _____

_____

Rules of Grammar

When composing a well-written paper, there should be many styles of sentences. One of
these is to begin a sentence with an *ing* word.

Example: Reading a book can really be exciting.

➥ Write a complete sentence that begins in a similar manner. _____

_____

Let's Have Some Fun!

➥ In the box to the right, Draw a figure 8 sideways. Now convert this into an animal. Your animal must have eyes, ears, nose, mouth, plus at least one other feature. Make your animal unique (different from anyone else's).

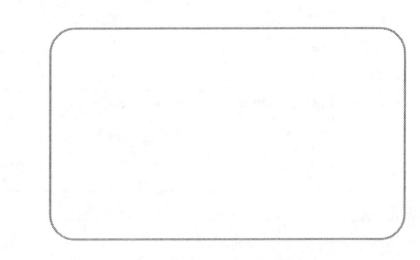

The Funnies

➥ What did the bee say to the rose?

Your Creative Answer: _____

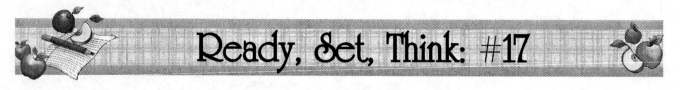

Quote of the Day

"A happy heart is better than a full purse."

~ Italian proverb

•❖ What does this proverb say to you? _____

_____

•❖ What are the ways to keep a happy heart? _____

_____

Rules of Grammar

One use of the apostrophe is to form the possessives of nouns. To form the possessive of a singular noun you must add an *'s*.

Example: The *boy's* hat is blue. (This says that one boy owns a blue hat.)

If a singular noun ends in *s* you still add an *'s*.

Example: *Charles's* book is missing. (The book that belongs to Charles is missing.)

•❖ Write one sentence in which you show ownership of a singular noun that does not end in *s*.

_____

_____

•❖ Now write a sentence in which you show ownership of a singular noun that ends in *s*.

_____

_____

What If?

•❖ What if you were born old and grew young? _____

_____

_____

_____

The Funnies

•❖ Who judges baking contests?

Your Creative Answer: _____

_____

Ready, Set, Think: #18

Quote of the Day

"If there is no struggle, there is no progress."
~ Ralph Waldo Emerson

→ What is struggle? _____

_____

→ What is progress? _____

_____

→ What does his quote say to you? _____

_____

Rules of Grammar

To form the possessive of a plural noun, you add an *'s* if the word does not end in *s* and add only an apostrophe if the plural ends in *s*.

Example: The third grade *girls'* party was canceled. (This says that there is more than one girl in the third grade (plural), and their party was canceled.)

Example: The store had *men's* hats on sale. (*Men* is plural but does not end in *s* so an *'s* must be added.)

→ Write two sentences using possessive forms. One should use a plural that ends in *s* and the other should use a plural that does not end in *s*.

1. _____

_____

2. _____

_____

Did You Say "Four"?

→ Think of all the ways to say *four*. Make a list. _____

_____

Famous Pairs

→ Fill in the blanks with the well-known missing partner.

Come and _____

In and _____

Cookies and _____

The Funnies

→ What is the poorest plant?

Your Creative Answer: _____

Quote of the Day

"Everyone must row with the oar he has."
~ English proverb

- Does this quote have anything to do with a boat?_____
  _____

- What is the analogy used in this proverb?_____
  _____

- What oar or oars have you been given? _____
  _____

Rules of Grammar

Do not begin a sentence with a numeric number. Instead, write out the number.

Example: Twenty-five people attended the meeting.

- Write a correct sentence that begins with a number._____
  _____

The Eyes Have It

- List all occupations (jobs) that you can think of that would not require eyesight.
  _____

- Write a poem that a pair of contacts or glasses might have written about their job.

  _____
  _____
  _____
  _____
  _____
  _____
  _____

The Funnies

- What is the laziest mountain in the world?

  Your Creative Answer: _____

  _____

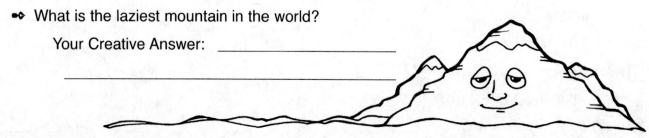

Quote of the Day

"We are all ignorant . . . only about different things."
~ Will Rogers

⚬ What does this quote mean? _____

_____

⚬ What is something that you are smart about? _____

_____

⚬ What is something that you would consider yourself to be ignorant about? _____

_____

Rules of Grammar

The titles of books, magazines, newspapers, paintings, and the names of ships should be underlined when written. When typing a sentence, italics can be used in place of underlining.

Example: We have just read <u>Mrs. Frisby and the Rats of NIHM.</u>

　　　　　We have just read *Mrs. Frisby and the Rats of NIHM.*

⚬ Write an original sentence using the name of a book, magazine, newspaper, painting, or ship. _____

_____

Goals

⚬ What is your goal for today? _____

_____

⚬ What is your goal for this week? _____

_____

⚬ What is your goal for your life? _____

_____

Complete the Thought:

⚬ I would like to have a dozen _____

_____

The Funnies

⚬ What would you get if you crossed a stereo with a refrigerator?

　　Your Creative Answer: _____

Quote of the Day

"Chance favors only the prepared mind."
~ Louis Pasteur

➡ What is another word for *chance*? _____

_____

➡ What does this quote mean? _____

_____

Rules of Grammar

The next few lessons we are going to study *homonyms*—words that sound the same but are spelled differently and have different meanings. You should know the difference between the words both in meaning and spelling.

➡ What do these words mean?

aisle_____

isle _____

altar_____

alter_____

arc _____

ark _____

What If?

➡ What if every time it rained all the cars melted and had to be kept under a roof?

_____

_____

➡ What if pennies were the only form of U.S. money? _____

_____

The Funnies

➡ What do you get when two strawberries meet?

Your Creative Answer: _____

_____

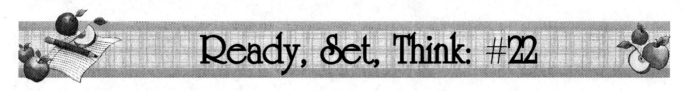

Ready, Set, Think: #22

Quote of the Day

"Vision is the art of seeing things invisible."
~ Jonathan Swift

- We often describe good leaders as people with a vision. What do we mean by this description? _____
  _____

- How does the above idea relate to the quote? _____
  _____

- Now that you have thought about vision and leadership, what does the quote mean?
  _____
  _____

Rules of Grammar

- Tell the meaning of each word.

  blew_____

  blue _____

  brake _____

  break _____

- Now, give a word that fits each definition. The two words will be homonyms.

  a grain food usually eaten at breakfast _____

  something repeating itself in a cycle _____

Major Rivers

- Name a major river in each of these places.

  Africa _____ U.S. _____

  Brazil _____ England_____

The Funnies

- How can you keep a barking dog quiet?

  Your Creative Answer: _____

Quote of the Day

*"Speak when you are angry, and you will make
the best speech you will ever regret."*
~ Ambrose Bierce

➥ What do you think this quote is saying? _____

_____

➥ Do you agree with it? Why? _____

_____

Rules of Grammar

➥ Write a homonym for each definition. For the last two, write the definition of each.

just _____

admission cost _____

postal delivery_____

a man _____

pore_____

pour_____

Fun Time

➥ Make a caption for this picture. Write it on the lines next to the cartoon.

The Funnies

➥ How did the blind carpenter get his sight back?

Your Creative Answer: _____

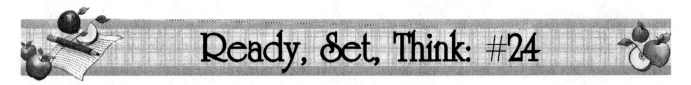

Ready, Set, Think: #24

Quote of the Day

"If we want to work out a policy for the present,
we must examine the past and prepare for the future."
~ Livy

•◆ How do we go about examining the past?_____
_____

•◆ What does this quote mean? _____
_____

Rules of Grammar

•◆ Give two examples of different times you must use an apostrophe. Then write a
sentence using an apostrophe for each case.

Rule 1: _____

Rule 2: _____

Sentence 1: _____

_____

Sentence 2: _____

_____

Wind Put to Poetry

•◆ Write a poem about the spring winds.

_____
_____
_____
_____
_____
_____

The Funnies

•◆ What was Batman doing in a tree?

Your Creative Answer: _____

Section 2: Quest for Your Best!

Section 2 is the midpoint for the student as he/she develops thinking skills for creative thought and problem solving. The format will remain similar and thus, familiar and comfortable for the students. Many of the concepts covered in Section 1 will be covered in Section 2, but the new concepts that have been added are listed below.

- **Idioms**—Idioms are phrases which society develops and understands, but the words have a meaning that is different from the literal meaning. To truly understand a language, one must understand its idioms.

- **Spelling Rules**—Each lesson includes a spelling rule with examples and a brief opportunity to practice it.

- **Joke of the Day**—This is the same as The Funnies in Section 1 and gives the student an opportunity to be creative and play with words as he/she **creates a new** answer.

- **Analogies**—These deal with relationships, which can be obvious or not so obvious. Solving analogies is definitely an exercise in higher ordered thinking.

- **Transformation**—This is a creative activity in which the student will transform one object into a totally different object.

- **Career Exploration**—This is an exposure activity which hopefully causes the student to think of his/her future and the opportunities available as a career.

- **Oxymoron**—An oxymoron is a combination of contradictory words that create an epigrammatic effect. Example: jumbo shrimp

- **Alliteration**—The repetition of sound for an auditory effect in writing of prose or poetry is a valuable skill for creative writing. Example: *Quips, Quotes, & Queries*

- **Word History**—This deals with how the meanings of our words derive from other languages or cultures in history.

- **Palindromes**—This is a word, phrase, sentence, or number that reads exactly the same both forward and backward. Example: racecar

- **Problem Solving**—Developing skills needed for solving problems cannot be overrated.

- **Personification**—Giving human traits or feelings to an inanimate object is a descriptive tool when writing creatively.

- **Triplets**—These are words that usually associate together. Example: bacon, lettuce, and tomato

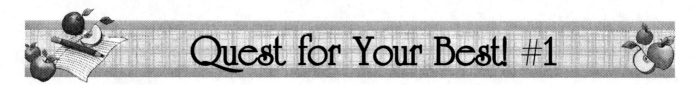

Quest for Your Best! #1

Quote of the Day

Our quote today is a common idiom. *Idioms* appear in every language. They are often confusing because the meaning of the whole group of words taken together has little, often nothing, to do with the meaning of the words taken one by one. In order to understand a language, you must know what the idioms in that language mean.

If an expression becomes overused, we call it a *cliché*, and many of the sayings we will study are clichés. Once these expressions were fresh and original, but today they are stale and trite. You should try to avoid using clichés in your own writing (unless you can put an imaginative new twist on them). You will hear and read clichés all the time.

*I don't know how Sally is going to persuade her mom to let her go shopping, but I'm sure she has an **ace up her sleeve**.*

- Write in a complete sentence what you think the idiom "ace up [your] sleeve" means.

_____

_____

- Where do you think this idiom might have started? _____

_____

Rules to Spell By

Rule: If the only vowel in a word is at the end, the vowel usually has a long sound.

- Think of five words that follow this rule. _____

_____

- Write a four-line poem with one of the above words at the end of each line. Do not repeat ending words. _____

_____

_____

_____

Joke of the Day

For each joke of the day, you should think of a new, clever answer. This activity will help you learn to have fun "playing" with words.

- Why did the turtle cross the road?

    Your Creative Answer: _____

_____

Quest for Your Best! #2

Quote of the Day

"It is easier to stay out than get out."
~ Mark Twain

- Write what you think the quote means. _____
  _____

- How can you apply this to your life? _____
  _____

- List five things it is easier to stay out of rather than get out of.

  1. _____
  2. _____
  3. _____
  4. _____
  5. _____

Rules to Spell By

Rule: When the letter *i* is followed by the letters *gh*, the *i* is usually long and the *gh* is silent.

- List three words that follow the rule.

  _____   _____   _____

- List one word that does not. _____

Sound

- Think of six words that rhyme with *face*.

  1. _____   4. _____
  2. _____   5. _____
  3. _____   6. _____

- Circle the one word you wrote that you think no one else thought of. Then, write a quick jingle or slogan for a sunscreen lotion using at least three of the words you listed.

  _____
  _____
  _____

Joke of the Day

- What do you call two bananas?

  Your Creative Answer: _____

Idiom of the Day

Molly is just giving you her dessert because she wants one of your puppies. ***Beware of Greeks bearing gifts***.

•➤ Do you think Molly is Greek? _____

_____

•➤ What do you think this idiom means? _____

_____

•➤ How and where do you think it might have originated? _____

_____

•➤ Think of a way you might use this expression. Write it here. _____

_____

Rules to Spell By

Rule: When *y* is the final letter in a word, it usually has a vowel sound.

•➤ Think of five words that follow this rule.

1. _____   4. _____

2. _____   5. _____

3. _____

•➤ Think of two words that do not follow this rule.

1. _____   2. _____

•➤ Now, create a fun poem using at least three words from above. _____

_____

_____

_____

_____

Joke of the Day

•➤ Why do elephants paint each of their toenails a different color?

Your Creative Answer: _____

Quote of the Day

"A horse never runs so fast as when he has other horses to catch up and outpace."

~ Ovid

- State what this quote means in your own words. _____
  _____

- Do you agree with this statement? Explain your answer. _____
  _____

- Who is Ovid? _____
  _____

Rules to Spell By

Rule: When *a* is followed by *r* and a final *e*, we expect to hear the sound heard in *care*.

- Think of three words that follow this rule.

  1. _____ 2. _____ 3. _____

- Now, think of one that doesn't follow the rule. _____

Analogies

- Write an analogy. Use one word from above in your analogy.

  _____ is to _____ as _____ is to _____

- Write an analogy using only pictures.

Greek Writing

- Now, write a sentence like the Ancient Greeks: no vowels, no spaces between words, and "as the ox plows." This means writing one line left to right and writing the next line backwards from right to left. It's fun! _____
  _____
  _____
  _____

Joke of the Day

- What kind of lights did Noah have on his boat?

  Your Creative Answer: _____

Quote of the Day

"Let everyone sweep in front of his own door and the whole world will be clean."
~ Johann Wolfgang von Goethe

• Write a complete sentence explaining what this quote means to you. _____

_____

• Do you think this quote is talking about brooms, vacuum cleaners, and dirt around your door? To what else could it relate? _____

_____

• How could you apply this quote in your everyday life? _____

_____

Rules to Spell By

Rule: *ch* is usually pronounced as it sounds in *kitchen*, *catch*, and *chair*—not like *sh*.

• Think of five words not listed above that follow this rule.

1. _____   4. _____

2. _____   5. _____

3. _____

• Think of at least one word that does not follow the above rule. _____

Transformation

• Make an animal from the number below by adding lines, curves, or features.

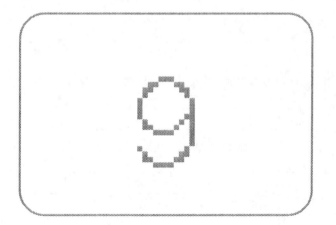

Joke of the Day

• What did the duck who was buying chapstick say to the drugstore clerk?

Your Creative Answer: _____

Idiom of the Day

Ms. Clark goes to college at night and works as a secretary during the day.
She's burning the candle at both ends.

↦ Does Ms. Clark burn candles dangerously while working her jobs? _____

↦ Is this referring to candles at all? What do you think it is really talking about? _____
_____

↦ Have you ever been in a situation where you might have been burning a candle at both ends? What was it? _____
_____

↦ How do you think this idiom may have started? _____
_____

↦ The common expression "burnout" comes from this. What does it mean to have "burnout?" _____
_____

Rules to Spell By

Rule: When *c* is followed by *e* or *i*, the sound of *s* is likely to be heard.

↦ Think of five words that follow the rule.

1. _____ 4. _____
2. _____ 5. _____
3. _____

↦ Now, think of one that does not. _____

Career Options

↦ Think of three jobs you could have as an adult that relate directly to our environment.

1. _____
2. _____
3. _____

British Spellings

↦ Write the American spelling beside the British spelling of each word.

1. axe _____
2. cheque _____
3. colour _____
4. flavour _____
5. waggon _____
6. pyjamas _____
7. civilise _____

Joke of the Day

↦ Use your wit to finish these sentences:

"I get up early," Tom said with _____.

"I am a burglar," Jim

Quest for Your Best! #7

Quote of the Day

"Success and failure are equally disastrous."

~ Tennessee Williams

• Tell in your own words what you think this quote might mean. _____

_____

• Why is failure sometimes disastrous? _____

_____

• Why is success sometimes disastrous? _____

_____

• Give an example of a disastrous success. _____

_____

• Does this quote always have to be true? Why or why not? _____

_____

Rules to Spell By

Rule: When the letter *c* is followed by *o* or *a* the sound of *k* is likely to be heard.

• Think of five words that follow this rule.

1. _____   4. _____

2. _____   5. _____

3. _____

• Write a sentence using two of these words. _____

_____

Career Options

• If you graduated from college with a degree in Communications, for what jobs might you qualify? Name four.

1. _____   3. _____

2. _____   4. _____

Colors

• Which color do you think is the happiest? _____

• Which one is the saddest? _____

Joke of the Day

• What do you draw without a pencil or paper?

Your Creative Answer: _____

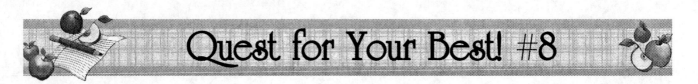

Idiom of the Day

*Janice **can't hold a candle** to Don when it comes to singing.*

- Is Janice trying to burn Don with a candle while he sings? _____

_____

- What do you think this idiom means? _____

_____

- Where and how do you think it might have originated?_____

_____

Rules to Spell By

Rule: The letter *g* often has a sound similar to that of *j* in *jump* when it precedes the letters *i* or *e*.

- Think of two words that follow this rule.

    1. _____

    2. _____

- Now think of one that does not.   _____

Rhyming Words

- Think of four words that rhyme with *spook*.

    1. _____   3. _____

    2. _____   4. _____

- Think of an unusual word that rhymes with *spook*, one that no one else is likely to think of.

_____

- Now write a three- or four-line poem using some of these rhyming words. _____

_____

_____

_____

Joke of the Day

- Use your wit to finish these sentences:

    "I'm a photographer," Tom said _____.

    "Step to the back of the boat," Jim said _____.

Quest for Your Best! #9

Quote of the Day

"To accomplish great things we must not only act but also dream, not only plan but also believe."
~ Anatole France

- What does this quote mean to you? _____

_____

- Do you think one of these (act, dream, plan, believe) is more important than the others?

_____

- Why is it important to act? _____

_____

...to dream? _____

_____

...to plan? _____

_____

...to believe? _____

_____

Rules to Spell By

Rule: When *ght* is in a word, *gh* is silent.

- Think of six words that follow the rule.

1. _____   4. _____

2. _____   5. _____

3. _____   6. _____

Oxymoron

An *oxymoron* is any combination of contradictory words that creates an epigrammatic effect. Two examples are "jumbo shrimp" (The *jumbo shrimp* on the menu were delicious) and "pretty ugly" (It was a *pretty ugly* scene when Jan was caught not telling the truth).

- Think of two other oxymorons:

1. _____   2. _____

Complete the Sentence

- What I want most in the world is _____

_____.

Joke of the Day

- When is a turkey scary?

Your Creative Answer: _____

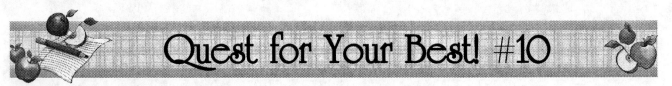

Idiom of the Day

*Taking books to the librarian's daughter is **like carrying coals to Newcastle**.*

- Does this mean the books are heavy? _____

  _____

- Does it mean they are a messy load? _____

  _____

- What do you think it means? _____

  _____

- Where did this idiom originate? _____

  _____

Rules to Spell By

Rule: When a word begins with *kn*, the *k* is silent.

- Think of three words that begin with *kn*.

  1. _____

  2. _____

  3. _____

Try This

- Write a sentence (minimum of five words) that makes sense with only words that end in r.

  _____

- Now, illustrate your sentence.

Complete This Sentence

- I am most thankful for _____

  _____

Did You Know?

The word *Sunday* comes from the Old English word "summandaeg." This meant "day of the Sun." The word *Monday* comes from Old English also, "monandaeg." This meant "day of the Moon."

Joke of the Day

- What language do turkeys speak?

Your Creative Answer: _____

Quest for Your Best! #11

Quote of the Day

"Success is just a matter of luck. Ask any failure."
~ Earl Wilson

- Mr. Wilson seems to be saying that failures are just making _____ for not succeeding. What is success? _____

    _____

- In your opinion, what are some main contributions to success? _____

    _____

- Do your agree with Mr. Wilson about those who have become "failures?" Explain your answer. _____

    _____

Rules to Spell By

Rule: When a word begins with *wr* the *w* is silent.

- List as many of the "wr" words as you can. _____

    _____

    _____

    _____

More About Your Week

Tuesday (from Old English—"tiwesdaeg"); day of Tiu, the god of war and the sky

Wednesday (from Old English—"wodenesdaeg"); day of Woden, the Teutonic god identified with Odin, the supreme deity in Norse mythology

Thursday (from Old English—"thur(e)s daeg"); influenced by the Old Norse "Thorsdagr" which means "day of Thor," the god of thunder in Norse mythology

Friday (from Old English—"frigedaeg"); day of Frigg, the wife of Odin and goddess of love in Norse mythology

Saturday (from Old English—"saeternaesdaeg"); Saturn's day (the Roman god identified with the Greek Titan who ruled the universe until overthrown by his son, Zeus, according to Greek myths)

Joke of the Day

- What do you call two dinosaurs about to burst into giggles?

    Your Creative Answer: _____

Idiom of the Day

*Bob's sister was caught **red-handed** sneaking a cookie from the cookie jar.*

• Do you think *Bob's* sister was embarrassed to be at the cookie jar with red hands?_____

• Were her hands red for another reason? _____

_____

• What do you think this saying means? _____

_____

• How might it have first started? _____

_____

Rules to Spell By

Rule: In most two-syllable words, the first syllable is accented.

• Give examples of three words that follow the rule.

1. _____ 2. _____ 3. _____

• Now give a word that does not: _____

Do You Remember?

• Most of our names of days came from what language? _____

Alliteration

When sounds are repeated in words for effect, it is called *alliteration*. Quite often this can result in a tongue twister.

• Write a sentence in which every word starts with the same sound as the beginning letter of your name. The longer, the better! _____

_____

• Illustrate your sentence.
in the box to the right.

Joke of the Day

• Who was left to dig at the archaeology site over the holiday?

Your Creative Answer: _____

Quest for Your Best! #13

Idiom of the Day

*Mary hid Bob's bike. That really **cooked his goose**.*

•➤ Was Bob's bike hot enough to cook a goose? _____

_____

•➤ What do you think this idiom means? _____

_____

•➤ How might this idiom have originated? _____

_____

Rules to Spell By

Rule: If the first vowel sound is followed by a double consonant, the first syllable usually ends after the first of the double consonants.

•➤ List five words that follow this rule. _____

_____

_____

Complete This Sentence

•➤ I like to eat at _____ because _____

_____.

Rhyming Words

•➤ List five words that rhyme with *folly*. _____

_____

_____

•➤ Now think of a word that you think no one else will list. _____

•➤ Write a holiday poem using these rhyming words. _____

_____

_____

_____

Joke of the Day

•➤ What do monkeys in the Amazon rainforest sing at Christmas?

   Your Creative Answer: _____

Quote of the Day

"Deep rivers move in silence, shallow brooks are noisy."

~ an old proverb

•❖ What do you think this quote means? _____

_____

•❖ Do you think this is true? Explain your answer. _____

_____

•❖ What analogy can you make from this quote? _____

_____

Rules to Spell By

Rule: If the last syllable of a word ends in *le*, the consonant preceding the *le* usually begins the last syllable.

•❖ List three words that follow this rule.

1. _____ 2. _____ 3. _____

•❖ *Buckle* is an example of one that does not follow the rule. Why do you think this one doesn't follow the rule? _____

Career Exploration

•❖ List three careers you could choose if you were interested in Marine Science.

1. _____ 2. _____ 3. _____

Complete This Sentence

•❖ I never want to forget _____

_____.

Alphabetical Foods

•❖ Give a food that begins with each letter given below.

A. _____   F. _____

B. _____   G. _____

C. _____   H. _____

D. _____   I. _____

E. _____   J. _____

Joke of the Day

•❖ What do you get when dinosaurs crash their cars?

Your Creative Answer: _____

Quest for Your Best! #15

Idiom of the Day

*Kate was **as cool as a cucumber** when she received the award from the governor of our state.*

- Why do you think a cucumber would be considered to be "cool"? _____

_____

- What does it mean that Kate was "cool"? _____

_____

- What might be the reason for this becoming an idiom? _____

_____

Rules to Spell By

Rule: When a word has only one vowel in it (not at the end), the vowel is likely to be short.

- List six words that follow this rule.

  1. _____   4. _____

  2. _____   5. _____

  3. _____   6. _____

- Give one word that does not follow this rule. _____

Rhyming Words

- List five words that rhyme with *bang*. _____

_____

- Give one word that you think no one else will think of. _____

- Write a short poem using the above words. Use as many of the words as you can.

_____

_____

_____

Complete This Sentence

- When someone hurts me, I _____

_____.

Joke of the Day

- Why did the stegosaurus wear his spikes to the party?

    Your Creative Answer: _____

Quote of the Day

"For sleep, riches, and health to be truly enjoyed, they must be interrupted."

~ Jean Paul Richter

➻ How can sleep be interrupted? _____

_____

➻ How can riches be interrupted? _____

_____

➻ How can health be interrupted?   _____

_____

➻ What do you think this quote means? _____

_____

➻ Do you agree? Explain your answer. _____

_____

Rules to Spell By

Rule: In a word of more than one syllable, the letter *v* usually goes with the preceding vowel to form a syllable.

➻ Think of one word that follows the rule.   _____

➻ Now, think of one that does not._____

Complete This Thought

➻ My favorite time of day is _____ because _____

_____.

Career Thoughts

➻ If you are good at math, list four jobs you could have as an adult. _____

_____

Strolling Vocabulary

➻ List as many words as you can that mean "to walk."_____

_____

_____

Joke of the Day

➻ What is the best way to communicate with a fish?

Your Creative Answer: _____

Idiom of the Day

It cost an arm and a leg to buy his ticket, but Mr. Baker really needed the vacation.

- Did Mr. Baker have to sell his arm and his leg to pay the price of a ticket? _____
- What do you think this idiom means? _____
  _____
- This idiom actually started in our country. Why do you think it got started? _____
  _____

Rules to Spell By

Rule: When a word has only one vowel letter, the vowel is likely to be short.

- Think of a word that is one syllable and the vowel is short for each vowel.

  (a) _____   (o) _____

  (e) _____   (u) _____

  (i) _____

Tools for the Job

- List at least six tools of an artist_____

  . . . six tools of a gardener _____

  . . . six tools of a student _____

  . . . six tools for the kitchen _____

  . . . six tools for the dentist_____

Think Time

- I would rather read than _____
  _____.
- The thing I like to do least is _____
  _____.

Joke of the Day

- A couple opened a tearoom, and it was an immediate success. After a time, though, they got greedy. They skimped on the ingredients, reused the tea bags, and sold stale food. Soon their customers deserted them and they went bankrupt. What is the moral of this story?

  Your Creative Answer: _____

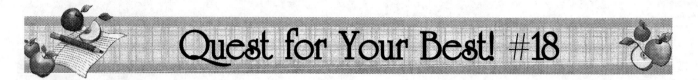

Idiom of the Day

*Don't stay home from the movies just because your best friend wants to go somewhere else with someone else. Why **cut off your nose to spite your face**?*

•> Are you so mad that you are going to cut off your nose? _____

_____

•> What do you think this means? _____

_____

•> This started in Rome in the 1200s. How do you think it was used originally? _____

_____

Rules to Spell By

Rule: When *y* or *ey* is seen in the last unaccented syllable, the long sound of *e* is heard.

•> List five words that fit this rule. _____

_____

_____

Pairs

•> These are some famous pairs. See how many you can think of after my first three clues.

Green Eggs and _____

Bacon and _____

Meat and _____

Did You Know?

Plastic six-pack holders are almost invisible underwater so animals can't avoid them.

•> How could this pose a problem for sea animals, water birds, or even humans? List as many problems as you can think of. _____

_____

•> Give a possible solution, other than just not throwing them in the water. _____

_____

Joke of the Day

•> What do you call crazy pickles?

Your Creative Answer: _____

Idiom of the Day

The dog days of summer *send you looking for a fan or air conditioning.*

• Do dogs need fans and air conditioning to keep cool in the summer? _____

_____

• Do people play with their dogs, get hot, and need air conditioning more in the summer?

_____

_____

• Where do you think we got this expression? _____

_____

• What do you think it really means? _____

_____

Rules to Spell By

Rule: An *r* gives the preceding vowel a sound that is neither long nor short. This is called an "*r*-controlled vowel."

• Think of four words in which the *r* controls the sound of the vowel in such a way that it is neither a long vowel sound nor a short vowel sound.

   1. _____   3. _____

   2. _____   4. _____

• Now think of an exception to this rule. _____

Rhyming Sounds

• Spring is coming soon! Think of five words that rhyme with *spring*.

   1. _____   4. _____

   2. _____   5. _____

   3. _____

• Now write a poem about spring using some of the above words at the end of the lines as rhyming words. Be sure you have a pattern to your rhyming poem (such as *aabb*, *abab*).

_____

_____

Joke of the Day

• Why did Johnny eat a dollar?

   Your Creative Answer: _____

Idiom of the Day

Don't take any wooden nickels while you are visiting New York City.

➡ Where can you spend wooden nickels? _____

➡ Why would someone give you this warning?_____

_____

➡ What do you think this expression means? _____

_____

➡ How might this expression have started? _____

_____

Rules to Spell By

Rule: The first vowel is usually long and the second silent in the digraphs *ai, ea, oa,* and *oi.*

➡ Think of one word for each of these digraphs given above. The digraph can appear anywhere in the word:

(ai) _____ (ea) _____ (oa) _____ (oi) _____

➡ Do your words follow the rule? _____

Palindromes

A *palindrome* is a word, phrase, sentence, or number that reads exactly the same both forward and backward. An example is the word *radar* or the number *737.*

➡ Think of four examples. Only one example can be a number.

1. _____

2. _____

3. _____

4. _____

➡ Now think of the longest palindrome you can. _____

Complete the Thought

➡ When I was little I thought (or believed) _____

_____.

Joke of the Day

➡ What 10-letter word starts with gas?

Your Creative Answer: _____

48

Idiom of the Day

*When she invested in the new business, **her money went down the drain**.*

•❖ Was her money in the sink or tub? _____

_____

•❖ Where do you think her money went? _____

_____

•❖ What does this expression mean?_____

_____

•❖ How might this idiom have started? _____

_____

Rules to Spell By

Rule: Words having double *e* usually have the long *e* sound.

•❖ Think of four words with double *e* that have a long *e* sound.

1. _____   3. _____

2. _____   4. _____

•❖ Now, think of a word that has a double *e,* and the sound is not a long *e*.

_____

Analogies

Analogies are comparisons. Sometimes they are comparisons that show relationships.

•❖ Complete these analogies.

7 is to 84 as _____ is to 156

Gaggle is to geese as _____ is to whales.

•❖ Now create two analogies of your own.

_____ is to _____ as _____ is to _____

_____ is to _____ as _____ is to _____

Joke of the Day

•❖ Why did the chicken cross the road?

Your Creative Answer: _____

_____

Quote of the Day

"There is no pillow so soft as a clear conscience."
~ French proverb

•• What do you think a soft pillow has to do with a clear conscience? _____

_____

•• What do you think this proverb means?_____

_____

•• Do you agree? Why? _____

_____

Rules to Spell By

•• Give one word that has an "r-controlled vowel." _____

•• Give one word that ends in *y* or *ey* and has a long e sound at the end. _____

•• Give one two-syllable word that divides before a *v* in it. _____

Roman Numerals

•• Give the Roman Numerals for the numbers below:

50 = _____   1000 = _____

19 = _____   10 = _____

5 = _____   99 = _____

6 = _____   100 =_____

1 = _____   12 = _____

More Word Pairs

•• Fill in the following word pairs.

huff and _____   law and _____

scream and_____   nook and _____

thick and _____   peaches and_____

far and _____   prim and _____

sticks and _____   tar and _____

live and _____   cream and_____

Joke of the Day

•• What do you get when you cross a pig with a centipede?

Your Creative Answer: _____

Quote of the Day

*"There is no limit to what can be done—if it
doesn't matter who gets the credit."*
~ Anonymous

➥ Explain in your own words what you think this quote means. _____

_____

➥ Think of an example in real life where you could see this being an important quote to
remember? _____

_____

➥ Give a brief description of the situation. _____

_____

Rules to Spell By

➥ Write a rule you remember from our study. Then give one word that fits your rule.

Rule: _____

Example: _____

Personification

Personification is a statement in which a thing or quality is represented in human form. Two
examples from William Shakespeare are, "How sweet the moonlight sleeps upon this bank!"
and "I will instruct my sorrows to be proud."

➥ Underline the personification in each of the examples above and then create a sentence
that exemplifies personification. _____

_____

Questions

➥ What are three questions that a picnic table might ask a library table?

1. _____

2. _____

3. _____

Joke of the Day

➥ What would you get if a lawnmower ran over a bird?

Your Creative Answer: _____

_____

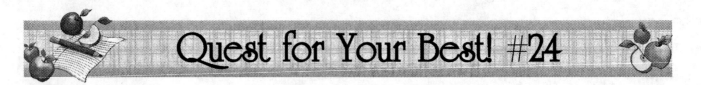

Quote of the Day

"Life is like a big red apple—only by taking a bite of it can I enjoy its crisp, juicy sweetness.
An apple can't be enjoyed to its fullest by sitting and watching it."

~ Anonymous

• Explain this simile. _____

_____

Problem Spellings

• The words below are frequently misspelled (but they are spelled correctly here).
Underline the part in the word that you think would be the problem and then use the
word in a well-developed sentence.

1. manila _____

2. necessary _____

3. oblige _____

4. occasion _____

5. occurred _____

Metric Conversions

1 inch = 2.54 centimeters	1 foot = 30.48 centimeters	1 yard = .91 meters

• Now, write a math problem in which you would need to know at least two of these
conversions. _____

_____

Question

• What is a question that an obtuse triangle might ask a parallelogram?

_____

_____

Joke of the Day

• What did the stamp say to the envelope?

Your Creative Answer: _____

Section 3: Thinking, For the Fun of It

After completing the first two sections, most students will have well-developed skills in higher-ordered thinking. The last section gives them the opportunity to actually have fun as they think creatively, flexibly, and fluently. Many of the concepts covered in the prior two sections will also be a part of Section 3. The students will truly be thinking for the fun of it. New concepts offered in this section are listed below.

- **Writing with Style**—This is a modeling activity in which students learn to write sentences using many and varied styles. The students who follow the plan show amazing growth at completion.

- **Metaphors**—The comparison of two unlike things without the use of "like" or "as."

- **Witty Words**—This is the equivalent of Joke of the Day and The Funnies in the prior sections. At this point, the students will be creative and clever as they play with words.

- **Analysis**—This is the skill of breaking a subject into smaller pieces to better organize it or better understand it.

Quote of the Day

"If you wouldn't write it and sign it, don't say it."
~ Anonymous

• What does this mean to you? _____

_____

• Have you ever said something you regretted? Explain. _____

_____

• Do you think this is a wise saying? Why?_____

_____

Writing with Style

Today we will start our sentences with *prepositional phrases*. A *preposition* shows relationships between its object and another word in the sentence. Here is an example:

"On the pleasant shore of the French Riviera, about halfway between Marseilles and the Italian border, stands a large, proud, rose-colored hotel." (F. Scott Fitzgerald)

• List the adjectives in this sentence: _____

_____

• Try your hand at writing a sentence that starts like this one._____

_____

Forced Association

• How is a baseball bat like a paper towel? _____

_____

Flexible Thoughts

• A muffin pan can be used for many things. List your 10 ideas. Circle the one you think will be different from anyone else's.

_____   _____

_____   _____

_____   _____

_____   _____

_____   _____

Witty Words

• Why did the farmer take the cow to the vet?

Your Creative Answer: _____

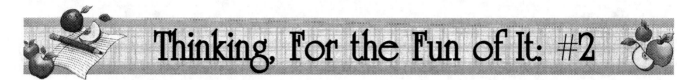

Thinking, For the Fun of It: #2

Quote of the Day

"Tis the set of the sail and not the gale, that determines the way it goes."

~ Anonymous

➥ This quote is an analogy. What do you think the analogy is? _____

_____

➥ What does this quote mean to you? _____

_____

➥ How can you apply this quote to your life? _____

_____

Writing with Style

Just off a cobblestone street in the drowsy, postcard city of Guernavaca, Mexico, sprawls a rambling, whitewashed hacienda.

➥ Write an original sentence using this same structure of prepositions and specific adjectives. Be creative! _____

_____

_____

What If?

➥ On the first day of school, you walked into your new classroom and found out that your teacher was the President of the United States. How would you feel about that?

_____

_____

_____

_____

_____

Witty Words

➥ What did one car muffler say to the other car muffler?

Your Creative Answer: _____

_____

Thinking, For the Fun of It: #3

Idiom of the Day

⟶ What is an idiom? _____

⟶ How is it different from a quote? _____

⟶ What is an idiom that you already know? _____

⟶ What does this idiom mean? _____

Writing with Style

Through a pleasant valley in the Ozark Mountains of Arkansas, about one hundred miles north of Hot Springs on Highway 7, flows a cool, crystal-clear, softly rippling stream.

⟶ Observe where commas are placed in this sentence. Why do you think they are necessary for a clear understanding of what the writer intended to say? _____

_____

⟶ Try your hand at writing a complex sentence in this pattern. Begin your sentence with a preposition. Be sure to use many descriptive words to elaborate and paint an exact picture in the readers' mind. _____

_____

Something to Think About

⟶ If you had to escort a visitor from outer space for a 30-minute tour of your town, where would your tour begin, what would it include, and where would it end? _____

_____

⟶ Is there any thing or place that you would intentionally omit? What would it be and why?

_____

_____

⟶ What would you like for him to tell his native people when he returned? _____

_____

How Much?

⟶ Fill in the blank for the conversion chart.

one mile = _____ feet   one mile = _____ yards

one mile = _____ kilometers   one mile = _____ meters

⟶ On the back of this paper, write a problem in which you need to know two of the above.

Witty Words

⟶ What song does a car radio play?

Your Creative Answer: _____

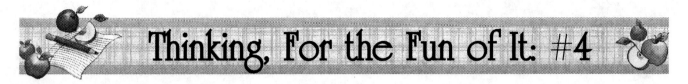

Thinking, For the Fun of It: #4

Idiom of the Day

*Mr. Johnson is a **dyed-in-the-wool** procrastinator*
and has never been on time in his life.

➡ Do you think Mr. Johnson has the word *procrastinator* dyed into his woolen clothes?

_____

_____

➡ What do you think this idiom means? _____

_____

➡ Try using this in an original thought and sentence. _____

_____

Writing with Style

"The lazy October afternoon bathed in a soft warmth of a reluctant sun,
held a hint of winter's coming chill." (Ruth Firor)

➡ Write three sentences like this in which you describe an afternoon, a morning, a house, a yard, or some other inanimate object. In your sentences, try "personifying" words such as "lazy" and "reluctant." _____

_____

_____

Meaningful Metaphors

A *metaphor* is a figure of speech in which one thing is compared to another to suggest that they are similar. You may not use the words *like* or *as*. Examples of metaphors are "A curtain of darkness fell over the city" and "A blanket of snow covers the city."

➡ Create a poem of at least four lines. Use an original metaphor in one of the lines.

_____

_____

_____

_____

That's a Good Question

➡ Which is more important: a promise or a mistake? Why? _____

_____

Witty Words

➡ What do you get if you cross an insect and a rabbit?

Your Creative Answer: _____

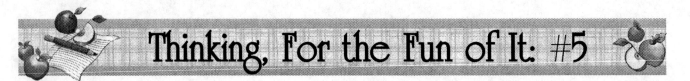

Idiom of the Day

*Cathy told me that learning how to cook is **as easy as rolling off a log**.*

➥ Is Cathy cooking on a log?_____

➥ What do you think she might think of rolling off a log? _____

➥ What do you think this idiom means?   _____

_____

➥ Where do you think this idiom might have originated? _____

_____

Writing with Style

The frail kite, tossed and battered by the March wind, took
one last dive and was swallowed by the tall grass.

➥ This sentence is a fantastic example of the effective use of personification in your writing. What do you know or remember about the meaning of personification? _____

_____

➥ How does personification make your writing more effective? _____

_____

➥ Write a well-developed sentence as the example above, using personification in more than one place. _____

_____

A Sticky Subject

➥ List 10 different uses for a smudge of peanut butter. (Be a flexible thinker.)

1. _____   6 _____

2. _____   7. _____

3. _____   8. _____

4. _____   9. _____

5. _____   10._____

The Answer Is . . .

➥ What is the question that goes with these answers?

1. a tornado _____

2. the zoo _____

3. Johann Bach _____

4. a right angle _____

5. soda _____

Witty Words

➥ Why did the man have to fix the horn on his car?

Your Creative Answer: _____

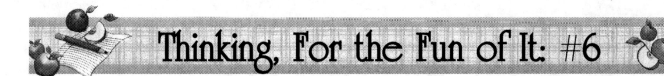

Thinking, For the Fun of It: #6

Idiom of the Day

*I made Tom **eat crow** by forcing him to admit that he was wrong.*

- Is Tom eating crow for dinner? _____

- Have you ever "eaten crow"?_____

  _____

- What do you think this saying means? _____

  _____

- Where do you think this idiom may have originated and why? _____

  _____

Writing with Style

The raging water, lashed by explosive spurts of wind,
battered the already crippled old freighter.

- This continues our practice in writing, using personification for effectiveness. Write a
  well-developed sentence that uses personification effectively. _____

  _____

Creativity with Math

- Write a poem about any area of math that you feel you understand well. It can be
  addition, subtraction, multiplication, division, fractions, decimals, geometry, rounding,
  estimation, etc. _____

  _____

  _____

  _____

- After you have written your poem, read the poem "Shapes" by Shel Silverstein. How is
  your poem like his poem? How is it different? _____

  _____

Witty Words

- Why shouldn't you tell a secret to a pig?

  Your Creative Answer: _____

  _____

Quote of the Day

"There's always free cheese in a mousetrap."
~ proverb

↦ What is another way of saying the same thing this proverb says? _____
_____

↦ Do you believe there is any truth in this proverb? Explain. _____
_____

↦ Create a new proverb that would mean the same thing. _____
_____

Writing with Style

↦ What is personification? _____
_____

↦ Why does the use of it in writing make the written word more effective? _____
_____

↦ Write an original sentence using at least two examples of personification. _____
_____

↦ Have you used it in any writing assignments outside of class since we have studied it?
_____

Proverbs to Go

A *proverb* is a wise saying. In the following activity, you should compose your own proverbs.
You will be given an open-ended sentence to complete. The sentence will contain a
homograph (a word with two or more meanings). After finding or thinking of two or more
meanings, select one of them and complete the sentence. Try to make the completed
sentence a proverb. For example, the phrase, "a bad round," could be completed as follows:

    1. A bad round *causes a boxer to lose points*.
    2. A bad round *could be returned to the butcher*.
    3. A bad round *may cause a gun to misfire*.

↦ Now it's your turn to try.

    1. Give him a sock and he'll _____
    2. Don't count your change _____
    3. If at first you don't express _____
    4. Hives make _____
    5. A refrain speaks louder _____

Witty Words

↦ When will paper make you itch?

    Your Creative Answer: _____

Idiom of the Day

*When Scott found out he had scored a goal for
the other team, he had **egg on his face**.*

- ◆ What do you think this idiom means? _____
  _____

- ◆ Do you think there was egg on the other team's goal? What does egg have to do with it?
  _____
  _____

- ◆ Where might this saying have originated? _____
  _____

Writing with Style

The example sentence given below has a participle, two verbs, and a simile.

> *"Streaming with perspiration, we swarmed up the rope and, coming into the
> blast of cold air, gasped like men plunged into icy water." (Conrad)*

- ◆ What is a participle? Use a dictionary or other resource book to help you. _____
  _____

Questions to Ponder

- ◆ In what ways can hot be cold? _____
  _____

- ◆ Which of your numbers would hurt the most if you were a touch-tone phone? Why?
  _____

The Alphabetical Orange Menu

- ◆ Think of as many orange foods as possible for the alphabetical list.

A: _____	J: _____	S: _____
B: _____	K: _____	T: _____
C: _____	L: _____	U: _____
D: _____	M: _____	V: _____
E: _____	N: _____	W: _____
F: _____	O: _____	X: _____
G: _____	P: _____	Y: _____
H: _____	Q: _____	Z: _____
I: _____	R: _____	

Witty Words

- ◆ What did one candle say to the other candle?
  Your Creative Answer: _____

Idiom of the Day

*Winning the spelling bee was quite a **feather in my cap**.*

- Was the prize for winning the contest a beautiful feather? If not, what do you think the statement meant? _____

  _____

- Where might this expression have originated? _____

  _____

- What is something that you have accomplished that was a feather in your cap?_____

  _____

Writing with Style

If you need to, look back at #8 to review what a participle is.

Straining with tension, I clambered up the castle wall and, coming in through the galley windows, shuddered like a man in his death rattle.

- Which of the words in this sentence are participles? _____

- With what letters do they end? _____

- What figure of speech is "shuddered like a man in his death rattle."_____

  _____

- Write a good sentence that begins with a participle, has two verbs, and a simile.

  _____

  _____

Word Plus Word

- Add one word to another word to make a third word.

  1. A large body of water + a male child = a period of time _____

  2. A lightweight bed of canvas + 2,000 lbs. = a type of fabric _____

  3. A vegetable + an edible kernel = a seed that ripens underground _____

  4. The nearest star + the antonym of *wet* = an adjective meaning several _____

  5. A rodent + a shade of brown = a plant used to make furniture_____

Think of a Great Answer

- What things are seen best with closed eyes? _____

  _____

Witty Words

- What kind of money do monsters use?

  Your Creative Answer: _____

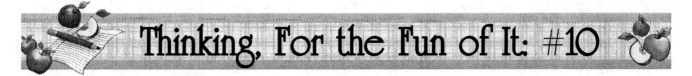

Quote of the Day

"If there is no wind . . . row!"
~ proverb

•◦ What does this proverb mean to you? _____

_____

•◦ How can you apply its meaning to your life? Be specific._____

_____

Writing with Style

Some sentences begin with participles.

> *Dripping with sweat, the horses lunged again and feeling the heavy load move, slowly freed it from the grip of the waxy black mud, like a tractor dragging the roots of an old tree from the soil.*

•◦ What is the simile in this sentence? _____

•◦ What are the participles? _____

•◦ How do participles usually end?_____

•◦ Does that mean that every word that ends that way is a participle? _____

•◦ Write a good sentence that begins with a participle and has a simile within it._____

_____

More Proverbs to Go

•◦ Using homographs, create more proverbs. Be sure to think of multiple meanings for words. This will help you be more creative.

1. Every cast _____

2. A party in need _____

3. Big enough to box _____

4. Let sleeping pupils _____

5. An idle park _____

Puzzling Punctuation

•◦ Which is more intelligent, a period or a question mark? _____

_____

Witty Words

•◦ What happened to the wolf who fell into the washing machine?

Your Creative Answer: _____

Idiom of the Day

> The banker **fiddled while Rome burned** as company bankruptcy loomed.

➻ Do you think this banker is a great musician? _____

_____

➻ Do you think he took a trip to Rome while conditions worsened?_____

_____

➻ What do you think he was doing while his bank was losing money? _____

_____

➻ Where do you think this idiom originated?_____

_____

Writing with Style

> *Even as she was falling asleep,* <u>*head bowed over the child*</u>,
> *she was still aware of a strange wakeful happiness.*

In the example sentence, the underlined section describes the "she" in the beginning of the sentence. Notice there are commas on both sides because it could be left out and still have a complete thought. Its purpose is to add elaboration and a better picture for the reader.

➻ Write an original sentence that is structured similarly to the one above. Be sure you have a complete thought without the section in commas._____

_____

Never Enough Time!

➻ If you could squeeze an additional hour into a 24-hour day, between what two hours would you squeeze the 25th? How would this extra hour help you? _____

_____

Pairs

➻ Complete the following pairs:

Lost and _____	Nuts and _____
Aches and _____	Pork and _____
Liver and _____	Hammer and _____
Safe and _____	Pins and _____
Tooth and _____	Touch and _____
Back and _____	Toss and _____
Mix and _____	Soup and _____

Witty Words

➻ What do you call a sleeping bull?

Your Creative Answer: _____

Idiom of the Day

*The teacher had to separate two students who were **fighting tooth and nail**.*

• What do you think to fight tooth and nail means? _____

_____

• Have you ever seen anyone fight tooth and nail? _____

_____

• Where do you think this expression came from? _____

_____

Writing with Style

As he swam toward the distant shore, head and shoulders lunging above the waves, the shark attacked and left a spreading crimson stain where the man had been.

• Underline the words in the sentence above that are adjectives.

• The words "head and shoulders lunging above the waves" describes the _____ in the beginning of the sentence. Why is this part of the sentence an effective part of the sentence? _____

_____

• Write a sentence that is structured similarly. _____

_____

Limited Vocabulary

• If you could have only 24 words in your vocabulary for the rest of your life, what words would they be?

_____ _____ _____ _____

_____ _____ _____ _____

_____ _____ _____ _____

_____ _____ _____ _____

_____ _____ _____ _____

_____ _____ _____ _____

• What word did you leave out that you felt like you really needed? _____

• If you were asked to write a story using only the words above, could you do it? _____

Witty Words

• What do you call a bee born in May?

Your Creative Answer: _____

Thinking, For the Fun of It: #13

Quote of the Day

"Duty is a matter of the mind. Commitment is a matter of the heart."

~ Anonymous

•➔ What is the difference between duty and commitment? _____

_____

•➔ How are duty and commitment alike? _____

_____

•➔ What is this quote saying? _____

_____

•➔ What is something you have as a duty? _____

_____

•➔ What is something for which you have felt a commitment? _____

_____

Writing with Style

As he sat before the doctor, his mangled hand dripping blood, the florescent light accented the pallor of his skin and the fear in his eyes.

•➔ What part of speech is each of the words listed below, adjectives or verbs?

sat _____ florescent _____

mangled _____ accented _____

•➔ If used differently in a sentence, could any of the four words above be another part of speech? Which ones, if any? _____

•➔ Write an original sentence with a descriptive clause set off in commas. _____

_____

Now We Write

•➔ Write a brief paragraph (at least five sentences) using only words from your word list of 24 in #12. _____

_____

_____

_____

_____

_____

Challenge

•➔ Write a sentence in which all the words begin with *t* (at least a five-word sentence).

_____

Witty Words

•➔ What kind of kitten works for the Red Cross?

Your Creative Answer: _____

Thinking, For the Fun of It: #14

Idiom of the Day

*Audiences thought she was going to be a great violinist,
but Cindy was just a **flash in the pan**.*

- ⚡ Do you believe that Cindy carried a pan with her for a part of her performances and created a flash of light? _____

- ⚡ Do you think she checked her looks in the reflection of a pan instead of a mirror?

  _____

- ⚡ What part do you believe a pan had to do with her playing the violin?

  _____

  _____

- ⚡ Where or how might this expression have started? _____

  _____

Writing with Style

- ⚡ From an ant's point of view, describe your pencil in a very detailed manner.

  _____

  _____

  _____

Timely Poetry

- ⚡ Write a poem about "time." It may be rhyming or non-rhyming.
  This poem must be at least four lines long and must have a rhyme
  or syllable pattern. Write what your pattern is after the poem.

  _____

  _____

  _____

  _____

  _____

Witty Words

- ⚡ What sickness do cowboys get from riding wild horses?

  Your Creative Answer: _____

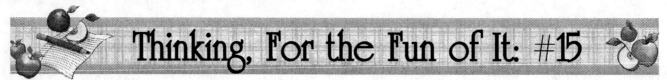

Idiom of the Day

*I guessed at most of the answers on the quiz. I was just **grasping at straws**.*

- Do you think the quiz was about plants such as grass and straw? _____
  _____

- Did the teacher have straws that you could reach for that had answers on them? _____
  _____

- Why was the quiz taker grasping for straws? _____
  _____

- How do you think this expression may have started? _____
  _____

Writing with Style

*Among the cabbage in the vegetable garden, about midway between the
first and second rows, sat a small but plump cottontail rabbit.*

- Write an original sentence that uses a similar sentence structure. _____
  _____

- How many describing words did you use?_____

- Which words in your sentence would you classify as vivid and specific? _____
  _____

Hitchhiking

- You have a very ordinary toothbrush. How could you use it for the following purposes?
  1. to teach a math lesson _____
  2. for a pet _____
  3. in the library _____
  4. during art _____
  5. during computer lab _____
  6. a gift for the principal _____
  7. as a birthday gift for an 11 year old _____
  8. in a lesson about the future _____

What If?

- What would happen if there were no more Saturdays? Make a long list. _____
  _____

Witty Words

- What did the big toe say to the little toe?

  Your Creative Answer: _____

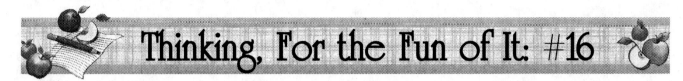

Idiom of the Day

*When Bob sees my new scooter, he'll be **green with envy**.*

• Is Bob allergic to scooters and will he become sick when he sees them? _____

• Is envy a disease? Explain. _____

_____

• What does this idiom mean? _____

_____

• How do you think this saying may have begun? _____

_____

Writing with Style

The butterfly, yellowish-gold, fluttered easily over the field of Black-eyed Susans.

• What is a more common word for *fluttered*? _____

• Why is *fluttered* a better choice for the sentence?_____

_____

• Where could you add one more describing word in this sentence? What would it be?

_____

• Write an original sentence with a similar structure that is even better than this sample sentence. _____

_____

Remembering the Past

• Who is your favorite explorer? Why? _____

_____

• What are some facts that you remember about this explorer? _____

_____

• What do you think is the most important trait of an explorer? Explain. _____

_____

Challenge

• Write a sentence (at least five words) in which every word that follows another must begin with the last letter in the word that preceded it. _____

_____

_____

Witty Words

• What did the dirt say to the rain?

  Your Creative Answer: _____

Quote of the Day

"Sometimes it is more important to discover what one cannot do than what one can do."

~ Lin Ytuang

•➔ What does this quote say to you? _____

_____

•➔ Why do you think it is important to know your weak traits as well as your strong traits?

_____

_____

•➔ What do you think is one of your strongest traits?_____

•➔ What do you think is one of your weak traits? _____

•➔ How should you feel about your weak traits? _____

_____

Writing with Style

After reading the example sentence, analyze the organization and punctuation of the sentence. Now write an original sentence using that format, style, and punctuation.

The wounded rabbit, red with blood, fell to rest on the warm, brown leaves.

•➔ Your original sentence with this pattern: _____

_____

Revisiting the Nursery Rhymes

•➔ Give the three most important things that happened in Humpty Dumpty's story.

1. _____

2. _____

3. _____

Questions, Questions?

•➔ What kind of adjustments would you have to make if everything you learned had to come from a book? _____

_____

•➔ Is there anything that you can only learn from written materials? What?

_____

Witty Words

•➔ If an athlete gets athlete's foot, what does an astronaut get?

Your Creative Answer: _____

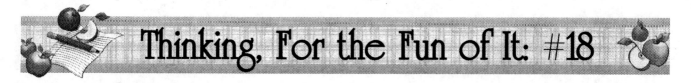

Quote of the Day

*"It is better to keep your mouth shut and appear stupid
than to open it and remove all doubt."*
~ Mark Twain

•◦ What does this quote say to you? _____

_____

•◦ Can you think of a time when you should have used this advice? When? _____

_____

Writing with Style

*The blue clouds, scattered about in an odd pattern, resembled
parts of a puzzle waiting to be put together.*

•◦ Your original sentence with this pattern: _____

_____

Poor Humpty Dumpty

•◦ List five ways that Humpty Dumpty might have been put together again.

1. _____
2. _____
3. _____
4. _____
5. _____

•◦ Now write a new verse for the nursery rhyme "Humpty Dumpty," using one of your above
ideas. _____

_____

_____

_____

Can You Do This?

•◦ Write a sentence in which each word ends in *ck*. _____

_____

Witty Words

•◦ What would happen if you ate yeast and furniture polish?

Your Creative Answer: _____

Thinking, For the Fun of It: #19

Quote of the Day

"Trifles make perfection, but perfection is no trifle."
~ Michelangelo

•◦ What are trifles? _____

•◦ Do you think that Michelangelo had to deal with trifles to become a great artist? _____

_____

•◦ What kind of trifles might an artist have to deal with? _____

_____

•◦ When have you had to deal with trifles to make something perfect? _____

_____

Writing with Style

The tired old man, dressed in his best Sunday suit,
walked slowly to church for the last time.

•◦ Your original sentence with this pattern: _____

_____

Sounds Like...

•◦ List as many sounds of alarm that you might hear. _____

_____

_____

Designs Just for You

•◦ Design a stamp in honor of your birthday. Make it very personalized.

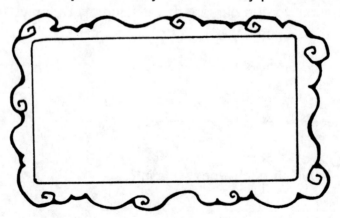

Witty Words

•◦ If a crow has one less pinion feather than a raven, how do you tell a crow from a raven?

Your Creative Answer: _____

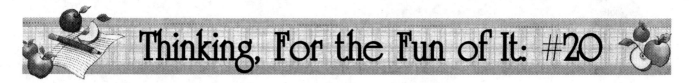

Quote of the Day

"Leadership is action, not position."
~ Anonymous

•• What qualities do you think of when you think of a leader? _____

_____

•• What is action? _____

_____

•• What is position? _____

_____

•• Put the meaning of this quote into your own words. _____

_____

Writing with Style

Rising from the ground, the water hose began to turn and swirling
in the air, wiggled like a snake preparing to strike.

•• Your original sentence with this pattern: _____

_____

_____

Graduating Tools

•• You are a wheelbarrow. Write a graduation speech for a class of building tools that are now ready to go into the world and do what they were designed to do.

_____

_____

_____

_____

Witty Words

•• If the Pilgrims came over on the *Mayflower*, how did the barbers arrive?

Your Creative Answer: _____

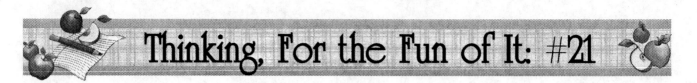

Thinking, For the Fun of It: #21

Quote of the Day

"When you play, play hard; when you work, don't play at all."

~ Theodore Roosevelt

- Be prepared to give your thoughts on this quote by a past president. _____

_____

- Do you live by this quote? Why or why not?_____

_____

Writing with Style

Grasping blindly for breath, he lurched for the life preserver and losing his grip, lunged under the angry, tumbling waters like a lifeless paper cup.

- Your original sentence with this pattern: _____

_____

The Lines Have It

- What would parallel lines say to a perpendicular line? _____

_____

More Sounds

- List all the sounds you can think of that might be heard in the jungle. _____

_____

_____

Habitats

- Would you rather live in a tree house or a cave? Give several reasons for your choice (both for and against). _____

_____

_____

Witty Words

- What was Noah's profession?

  Your Creative Answer: _____

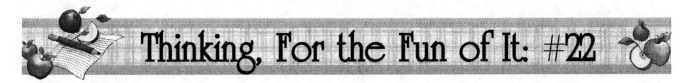

Quote of the Day

"Rudeness is the weak man's imitation of strength."

~ Eric Hoffer

➼ Restate this quote in your own words. _____

_____

➼ Do you agree with that statement? Why or why not? _____

_____

Writing with Style

➼ Review Quips 4–7, then write a sentence using personification and a participle. Underline describing words that are specific. _____

_____

_____

What Would You Rather?

➼ Would you rather be a cobweb or a fishnet? Why? _____

_____

➼ Would you rather be a picture postcard or a letter? Why? _____

_____

➼ Would you rather be the lettuce or the tomato on a sandwich? Why? _____

_____

Spring Colors

➼ What would the color green say about the color purple if green could talk. _____

_____

_____

Witty Words

➼ What did the painter say to the wall?

Your Creative Answer: _____

Thinking, For the Fun of It: #23

Quote of the Day

"A leader is at his best when people barely know he exists."

~ *Lao-tzu*

- ❧ What do you think this quote means? _____

  _____

- ❧ How can a leader lead quietly? _____

  _____

- ❧ Do you think of yourself as a leader? Why? _____

  _____

What If?

- ❧ What if a mother duck and her six babies began to trail you everywhere you went? Write a short story about an hour in your day with your new companions. Use some of the sentence patterns that we have been practicing this year in your brief history.

  _____

  _____

  _____

  _____

  _____

  _____

Witty Words

- ❧ Why do misers talk so little?

  Your Creative Answer: _____

Quote of the Day

"Brevity is the soul of wit."
~ William Shakespeare

• Who is William Shakespeare? _____

_____

• Why do you think we still read and study his literature in high schools and colleges?

_____

_____

• What does this quote mean? _____

_____

• Do you think Shakespeare may have been a man of brevity? Explain your answer.

_____

_____

Writing with Style

• Shakespeare was a master of personification. Personification is one of the tools we have studied this year that can help us write with style. Below, create a poem on any topic related to spring. Use personification at least once in your poem.

_____

_____

_____

_____

_____

Introductions

• How would a butterfly and a 727 jet introduce themselves to each other?

_____

_____

_____

Witty Words

• What did Cinderella say when her photos didn't show up?

Your Creative Answer: _____

Many questions are open-ended, and therefore, answers will vary. Accept reasonable and well-developed responses. Possible answers are given when appropriate.

Page 4 — Grammar: capital; different kinds of sentences require different ending punctuation.

Page 5 — Animal: elephant, tiger, rhinoceros, snake, eel. **Fun:** swallow; "pear-a-eat"

Page 6 — Quote: Aristotle was a Greek philosopher and scientist who lived from 384–322 B.C. **Grammar:** person, place, or thing; I, she, he, they, we, it, me, her, him, them, us, you. **Comparisons:** both offer protection, both have corners, both have entrances, both are made from a once living thing. **Rhyme:** beak, bleak, creak, freak, Greek, antique, boutique, critique, midweek, mystique, etc. **Fun:** at the meat ball; where the "moo"sic is

Page 7 — Quote: Edison was an inventor who lived from 1847–1931. **Collections:** colony, drift, pride, covey. **Fun:** diamond cutter

Page 8 — Grammar: (noun) person, place, or thing; (pronoun) takes place of a noun. **Finish:** saves nine, keeps the doctor away, flock together, waste, pound foolish, runs deep. **Fun:** they spend too much time in the dumps; their job stinks

Page 9 — Quote: Einstein was a genius and brilliant mathematician. **Celebrate:** Grandparent's Day, National Poetry Day, Mother-in-law Day, UN Day, Halloween, UNICEF Day, Apple Day, Fire Prevention Week, National Handicapped Employee Week. **Fun:** Mighty Mouse, King of Cheese

Page 10 — Quote: Helen Keller was the first blind/deaf person to earn a college degree. **Fun:** they fasten their sheet belts; they haunt the horn

Page 11 — Quote: An island is a body of land surrounded by water. **Abbreviations:** lb., in., ave., st., km., blvd., oz., qt., TX, Thurs., Response if it pleases you, Central Standard Time, Limited, miles per hour. **Fun:** his heart wasn't in it; he was a bonehead; he didn't have the guts

Page 12 — Quote: Longfellow was an American poet, educator, and a linguist who lived from 1807–1882. **Grammar:** (noun) person, place, thing; (pronoun) takes the place of a noun; (verb) states action, being, or state of being; (adjective) describes a noun or pronoun; (adverb) describes an adjective, a verb, or another adverb; (conjunction) a connecting word such as *and*, *or*, *but*, etc.; (interjection) expresses strong feeling. **Numerals:** X, I, V, L, C, XIX, XLIX, XCIX, II. **Math:** 21, 360°, no, 90°, distance around. **Fun:** trombone; bones; saxabone

Page 13 — Questions: 10, 100, 1000, 3000, Anno Domini. **Fun:** ground meat, grass potatoes

Page 14 — Grammar: what kind, how. **Fun:** evaporated milk

Page 15 — Corny: cornucopia; corner; cornet; cornea; corned beef. **Fun:** I've got you covered; you're a head of me; I thought eagles were bald!

Page 16 — Chart: goose, gander, gosling; bull, cow, calf; doe, buck, fawn; ewe, ram, lamb; sow, boar, piglet. **Fun:** he always "nicks" himself, he is "nickel-less" to buy razors

Page 17 — Threes: 1. Three Blind Mice; 2. The Three Bears; 3. The Three Billy Goats Gruff; 4. Three Little Pigs. **Fun:** so it would jingle all the weigh; for the meat bells; to ring up the price

Page 18 — Forest: elder, rubber, orange, pecan or walnut, locust, spruce, apple, ash, pine. **Fun:** a nightingale; a dark stormy night

Page 19 — Fun: "Hi, Bud!"; "Bee my honey"; "You look rosy"

Page 20 — Fun: "pie Rates" (pirates); the Friar; Brownies; the Fudge

Page 21 — Four: 3 + 1; 5 – 1; 2 x 2; quarter; quad; tetrad. **Pairs:** go; out; milk or cream. **Fun:** a vine because it can't support itself; poor-sin ivy; a "broke" tree

Page 22 — Fun: Mt. Everest; Himalayas

Page 23 — Fun: real cool music; radioactive food; juice box; cold rap

Page 24 — Fun: a strawberry shake; a "pear"; jam; straw babies

Page 25 — Rivers: Africa = Nile; U.S. = Mississippi; Brazil = Amazon; England = Thames. **Fun:** with hush puppies; with a sleeping pillow

Page 26 — Grammar fair/fare; mail/male; a minute opening; to cause to flow from one container to another. **Fun:** he picked up his hammer and saw; with an I-beam; seeing-eye log

Page 27 — Fun: looking for Robin; getting Poison Ivy; looking for Cat Woman

Page 29 — Idiom: In the 1500s, clothes did not have pockets, so people hid things in their sleeves. Magicians and dishonest card players both began to hide things in their sleeves. **Joke:** to get to the Shell station; to get to his girlfriend, Shelly's, house; to find the rabbit

Page 30 — Spelling: exception = neighbor; weigh. **Joke:** pair of slippers; an appealing couple.

Page 31 — Idiom: The great, ancient Roman writer Virgil used a similar expression in his famous story of the Trojan War. *The Aeneid* tells the story of the Greek trick at Troy as they brought in a huge horse as a gift, but it was filled with soldiers who captured the city after the "gift" was brought inside the city walls. **Spelling:** dry; tray; etc. **Joke:** so they can hide in the jellybean jar; so they could be the latest "phant."

Page 32 — Quote: Ovid was a great Roman poet who lived from 43 B.C. He is best known for his wit. **Spelling:** bare, dare, fare; are. **Joke:** flood lights; Israelites; skylights

Page 33 — Spelling: "ch"—catch, etc.; "sh"—machine. **Joke:** put it on my bill

Page 34 — Idiom: This is a French expression (ca. 1500). Sometimes people would burn a candle at both ends to get more light, but used up the candle faster. **Spelling:** "s" sound—cent; exception—cello. **British:** ax, check, color, flavor, wagon, pajamas, civilize. **Joke:** 1. "alarm" ; 2. "broke in"

Page 35 — Spelling: ("k" sound) coal. **Joke:** blinds; conclusions; closer

Page 36 — Idiom: In the 1500s a servant called a "link-boy" held candles for people. This was considered a lowly job; thus, it came to mean low value. **Spelling:** engine; give. **Joke:** "candidly," "in a flash"; "sternly," "waveringly"

Page 37 — Spelling: fight; daughter. **Oxymoron:** terribly good, loud whisper, sad smile. **Joke:** when he is a "goblin"

Page 38 — Idiom: There are already many coal mines in Newcastle, England. It's unnecessary to bring more there. **Spelling:** knife; knight.
Joke: gobble-ly-gook; Turkish

Page 39 — Spelling: write; wrap.
Joke: prehysteric; a pair of smiley faces

Page 40 — Idiom: originally referred to a person caught in a crime with blood on his hand—later referring to any wrong deed. **Spelling:** accented first syllable—famous, etc.; accented second syllable—polite.
Joke: the skeleton crew; Sandy Claws; St. Pick

Page 41 — Idiom: To spoil someone's plans. Medieval towns under siege would hang a goose outside the gate to say the enemy was stupid. The enemy might burn it and the town if angry enough. **Spelling:** bullet; rubber. **Joke:** "Jungle Bells"; "Deck the Trees"; "Oh, Swinging Tree"; etc.

Page 42 — Spelling: tumble; castle.
Joke: T-"wrecks"

Page 43 — Idiom: It has been known as early as the 1500s that the interior of a cucumber can be 20° cooler than outside. **Spelling:** hid; kind.
Joke: so he'd be a sharp dresser.

Page 44 — Spelling: follow—cover, etc.; doesn't follow—clover. **Joke:** drop him a line; get him hooked on you

Page 45 — Idiom: from early American wars; giving a leg or arm was a great sacrifice. **Spelling:** hat; pen; sit; dot; cut.
Joke: "Honest Tea" is the best policy

Page 46 — Idiom: From the 1200s when people would cut off their ugly nose only to have a disfigured face. Now, a spiteful response that harms you. **Spelling:** baby, money. **Pairs:** ham; eggs; potatoes.
Joke: Daffy Dills; coo-coo cumbers

Page 47 — Idiom: Rome, Sirus, the Dog Star, which rose in the hottest season. They thought the stars make it hot. **Spelling:** car, bird; hire. **Joke:** it was his lunch money; he liked rich food; so he could have a buck tooth

Page 48 — Idiom: In America, city slickers would fool country folk with wooden nickels. **Spelling:** (ai) wait; (ea) eat; (oa) boat; (oi) soil. **Palindromes:** "not a ton"; "pop"; "Go hang a salami. I'm a lasagna hog."
Joke: automobile

Page 49 — Idiom: Water can be a valuable item and even reused. When it goes down the drain, it is gone forever. **Spelling:** seem; been. **Analogies:** 13, pod.
Joke: for foul reasons

Page 50 — Numerals: L, XIX, V, VI, I, M, X, XCIX, C, XII. **Pairs:** puff, stones, cream, shout, let live or learn, proper, thin, order, feather, near or wide, cranny, sugar. **Joke:** Bacon & Legs; Pig with a s(cent)

Page 51 — Joke: shredded tweet; feather pillows

Page 52 — Joke: stick with me and we'll go places; let's get some ZIP

Page 54 — Style: pleasant, French, Italian, large, proud, rose-colored. **Association:** both can clean up; both made from a living thing. **WW:** It was too "moo" dy; It had hay fever

Page 55 — WW: Am I exhausted?; you need a new perfume

Page 56 — Idiom: (idiom) a common expression in which words usually do not mean what they say in a literal sense; (quote) the exact word someone spoke.
How Much?: 5,280 ft.,1.6 km, 1,760 yd., 1600 m. **WW:** cartoons; "car"aoke; heavy metal

Page 57 — WW: Bugs Bunny; grasshopper

Page 58 — Idiom: From loggers floating down river on logs. **WW:** it didn't give a hoot; it blew out; it had a stuffy honker

Page 59 — Idiom: War of 1821; American officers were forced to eat dead crow for doing wrong. **WW:** he'll squeal; he'll "tail" on you

Page 60 — Style: giving life-like traits to an inanimate object; paints a more precise and vivid picture with words. **WW:** scratch paper

Page 61 — WW: going out tonight?; you blew it

Page 62 — Word Plus: 1. season; 2. cotton; 3. peanut; 4. sundry; 5. rattan. **WW:** weird dough; GRReen

Page 63 — WW: became a "wash and wear-wolf"; was brain washed; tangled with a red hood

Page 64 — Idiom: In 64 A.D. Emperor Nero stood on a high tower and played his fiddle (lyre) while he watched Rome burn. **Pairs:** found, pains, onions, sound, nail, forth, match, bolts, beans, nails, needles, go, turn salad **WW:** a non "moo" ver

Page 65 — Idiom: Wild animals fight with their teeth and their claws. This started as a Latin proverb. **WW:** a maybe; a May son

Page 66 — Style: verb, adjective, adjective, verb, yes, mangled, accented. **WW:** first-aid kitten; a crossbreed

Page 67 — Idiom: On a 1600s flintlock musket, the gunpowder sometimes would only make a flash instead of explode. **WW:** bronchitis; a hoarse cough

Page 68 — Idiom: Ancient people would clutch frantically for reeds in the river, when drowning. **WW:** There's a big heal following you!; Why did you cry all the way home?

page 69 — Idiom: Shakespeare associated green with jealousy. He referred to it as the "green sickness" in his play *Antony and Cleopatra*. **WW:** If this keeps up, my name will be mud; I'm all washed up, thanks to you.

Page 70 — WW: mistletoe; lunar leg

Page 71 — WW: rise and shine; I'd be bright and make the honor roll

Page 72 — WW: It's just a matter of a pin-ion; from their "tales"

Page 73 — WW: on clipper ships; they took a short cut

Page 74 — WW: "ark"-itect; "ark"-eologist; zookeeper

Page 75 — WW: One more crack like that and I'll plaster you; You sure need another coat

Page 76 — WW: they don't want to put their two cents in; talk is cheap; he was told to put his money where his mouth was

Page 77 — WW: one day my prints will come; I can't wait to see my prints

Skills and Strategies Index